12/14

W9-BRF-553

SUPER
SOCIAL STUDIES
INFOGRAPHICS

ECONOMICS THROUGH INFOGRAPHICS

Karen Latchana Kenney

graphics by
Steven Stankiewicz

Lerner Publications Company
Minneapolis

Lerner Publications Company
A division of Lerner Publishing Group, Inc.
241 First Avenue North
Minneapolis, MN 55401 USA

For reading levels and more information, look up this title at
www.lernerbooks.com.

Main text set in Univers LT Std 12/15.
Typeface provided by Adobe Systems.

Library of Congress Cataloging-in-Publication Data

Kenney, Karen Latchana.
    Economics through infographics / by Karen Latchana Kenney ;
illustrated by Steven Stankiewicz
        p.   cm. — (Super social studies infographics)
    Includes index.
    ISBN 978–1–4677–3460–8 (lib. bdg. : alk. paper)
    ISBN 978–1–4677–4745–5 (eBook)
    1. Economics–Juvenile literature. I. Stankiewicz, Steven,
illustrator. II. Title.
HB183.K46 2015
330–dc23   2013037679

Manufactured in the United States of America
1 – PC – 7/15/14

CONTENTS

THE MONEY TRAIL

Do you have the makings of a financial whiz? To find out, take this pop quiz.

1. Do you wonder how much the minimum wage has gone up since your grandparents were kids?

2. Do you ever think about how many Israeli shekels are equal to a US dollar?

3. Have you looked up where your favorite jeans were made?

4. Are you curious about the cost of an iPhone in Russia?

Did you answer yes to any of those questions?

$$$$

CONGRATULATIONS!

You've got what it takes to uncover the secrets of economics. Every day, all around the world, products are made, bought, and sold. Money is spent and saved. People go to work. All these activities help make up an economy.

Economists use charts, graphs, and other infographics to make sense of economic processes. These tools can help you understand the different ways money is used—and how it shapes our lives.

Are you ready to take a trek down the money trail? From trading and currency to Furbies and Big Macs, economics is full of surprises. Read on to find out more!

A FAIR TRADE

When we think of money, paper bills and metal coins come to mind. But people have been buying and selling things since long before those forms of currency existed. How? By trading items for other items of roughly the same value. This practice was called bartering.

What's a rodent worth? A *lot* to early European colonists in North America. Beaver fur was the hottest trend in fashion. But European money had little value in the American wilderness, so the pelts (skins and fur) of this large rodent were traded for goods instead. Here's what a large beaver pelt could buy in goods.

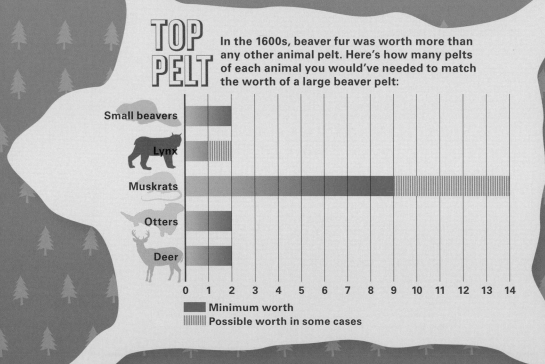

TOP PELT

In the 1600s, beaver fur was worth more than any other animal pelt. Here's how many pelts of each animal you would've needed to match the worth of a large beaver pelt:

- Small beavers
- Lynx
- Muskrats
- Otters
- Deer

0 1 2 3 4 5 6 7 8 9 10 11 12 13 14

■ Minimum worth
▓ Possible worth in some cases

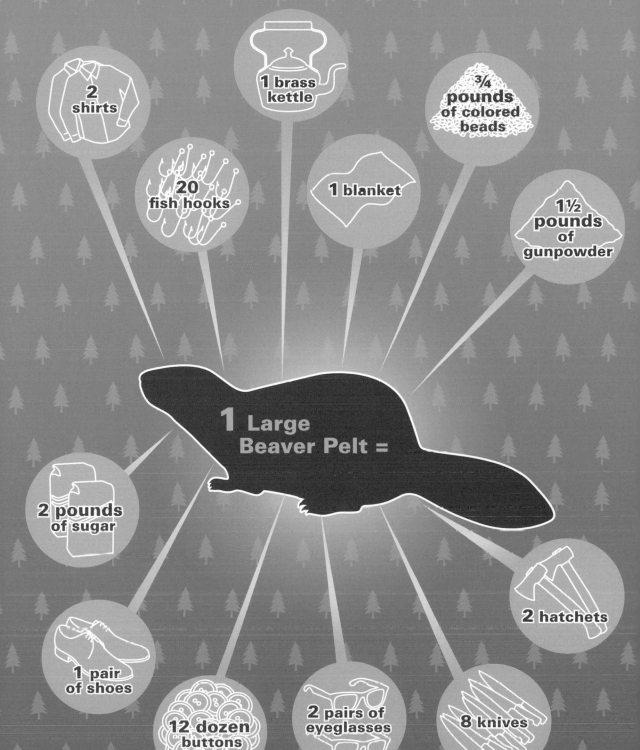

2 shirts

1 brass kettle

¾ pounds of colored beads

20 fish hooks

1 blanket

1½ pounds of gunpowder

1 Large Beaver Pelt =

2 pounds of sugar

2 hatchets

1 pair of shoes

12 dozen buttons

2 pairs of eyeglasses

8 knives

FOLLOW THE ECONOMY

What exactly *is* an economy? It's not a thing, really—it's more of a process. It defines how goods are made, sold, and bought in a country. There's more than one type of economy. A free market economy is controlled by people and their needs. A planned economy depends on the government. Check out how each kind of economy works.

AUSTRALIA HAS A FREE MARKET ECONOMY

People buy and use goods.

Businesses make and supply more goods.

People buy and use more goods.

The prices of goods are based on demand (how many people want the goods) and supply (how many goods exist and can be sold). Goods in high demand and low supply cost more. Goods in low demand and high supply cost less.

Businesses compete for buyers. This leads to lower prices.

People usually have a constant supply of most goods at low prices.

NORTH KOREA HAS A PLANNED ECONOMY

The government decides how many goods will be made. The government also sets the prices for the goods.

Businesses make the number of goods assigned to them.

Stores receive certain amounts of goods.

People buy the goods at government-set prices.

If demand is low, people have a supply of the goods at a fixed price.

If demand is high, the goods may sell out. There is no more supply left.

Businesses are not allowed to make more goods. Goods cannot be bought. There may be a shortage.

LET'S EXCHANGE!

Going somewhere? Well, if you're heading to another country, you'll need to use that country's currency. You can't buy chicken satay in Thailand with Mexican pesos!

Most countries have their own currency—government-issued bills or coins used to buy goods. But not all currency has the same value. One US dollar is worth a lot more than one Indian rupee. You can't just substitute one for the other. So tourists have to swap their money for the currency of the country they're visiting. In exchange for their stacks of bills, they'll get the same value in local currency—though it might look like more or less. Here's how a US dollar stacks up in value with other currencies around the world:

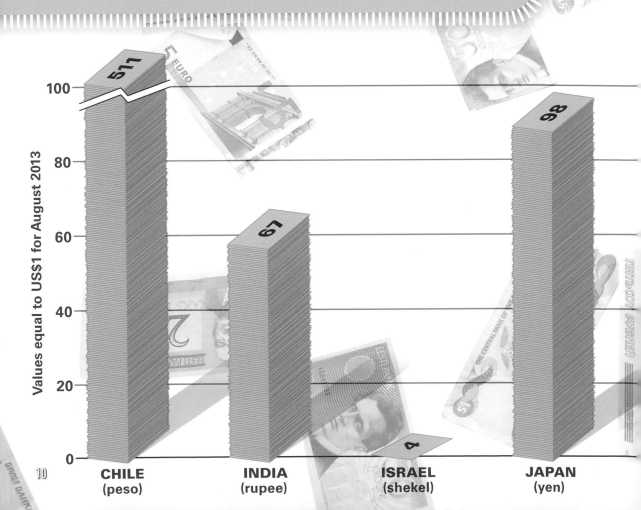

Values equal to US$1 for August 2013

- CHILE (peso): 511
- INDIA (rupee): 67
- ISRAEL (shekel): 4
- JAPAN (yen): 98

FLOATING VALUES

Many currencies change in value. Sometimes values float up, and sometimes they sink way down. Lots of factors affect a currency's value. If the currency is in high demand around the world, it can go up in value. Here's how the European Union's euro changed in value from 2012 to 2013:

Values in US dollars

1.35	
1.30	
1.25	
1.20	

1.3644

1.3302

1.3406

1.2993

1.3266

1.2768

1.2545

August 29, 2012
October 31, 2012
December 19, 2012
February 1, 2013
March 27, 2013
June 19, 2013
August 29, 2013

13

10

7

32

MEXICO
(peso)

SOUTH AFRICA
(rand)

SWEDEN
(krona)

THAILAND
(baht)

GOTTA HAVE IT!

Some items are in high demand. People just *have* to have them. For instance, certain toys have been really hot sellers through the years. These toys flew off the shelves as soon as they were stocked. Sellers couldn't keep enough supply to sell to every customer. When buyers found the few toys for sale, they paid just about anything to get them.

Prices can go sky-high during a toy craze. People who've already bought the toys can resell them for extreme amounts. See how high the resale prices got for some of the all-time hottest-selling toys.

RESALE PRICE: up to $4,000

CABBAGE PATCH KID
1980s
Store price: $20–$50

RESALE PRICE: more than **$100**

FURBY
1990s
Store price: $30–$35

RESALE PRICE: up to **$2,000**

TICKLE ME ELMO
1990s
Store price: $29

RESALE PRICE: **$32–$36**

ZHU ZHU PET
2000s
Store price: $8–$9

ON THE ASSEMBLY LINE

Ready to go into business? You could make a product to sell. But first, you'll need raw materials, money to buy them, and people power. Then you'll need to decide how to use these resources. It's important to weigh the costs and benefits carefully. Businesses can be expensive to start and even more expensive to run. You have to be sure that in the end, you'll gain more than you lose.

Carmaker Henry Ford was a whiz at balancing costs and benefits. He used his resources wisely. He made cars better, faster, and more cheaply than any other car company. Here's how he did it:

PRE-MODEL T

Skilled craftsmen make car parts. They assemble the parts to make a car. It takes a long time to make one car. Cars are also very expensive to buy.

1908

The Model T car is produced. It sells so well that the factory cannot keep up with the orders.

1901

The Olds Motor Works uses the first assembly line to build cars. This speeds up production.

1903

Ford creates the Ford Motor Company. He wants to make cars for everyday people, not just the rich.

1913

Ford's factory starts using a moving assembly line. Car parts sit on conveyor belts that take them from worker to worker. Workers make cars much faster than before.

1914

Ford raises the pay for his workers to $5 for an eight-hour day. This is twice the pay that other carmakers offer. More workers want jobs at Ford's factory.

1917

Ford begins building his Rouge factory complex. Here, he will produce the materials he needs to make his cars, such as steel, tires, and batteries. This cuts his costs. He can then make more profit.

1930s

More than 100,000 workers are employed at the Rouge factory complex. One new car is completed every 49 seconds at the factory.

FASTER AND FASTER

See how the moving assembly line sped up the time it took to make one car.

UNMOVING ASSEMBLY LINE — 12 hours, 8 minutes

MOVING ASSEMBLY LINE — 1 hour, 33 minutes

Hours: 0   2   4   6   8   10   12

TOTALLY GLOBAL

You're an expert on that awesome new game system, right? Did you know it was made in China? Today's market is totally global. Goods are made and sold in just about every part of the world. Countries export some of their goods to buyers in other countries. Take a look at some top exporters of goods around the world. Check out some of the goods they make and see which countries buy those goods.

CHINA
VALUE OF EXPORTS: $2.1 trillion
GOODS MADE: computer equipment, clothing, telephone parts
TOP CUSTOMERS: United States, Hong Kong, Japan, South Korea

UNITED STATES

FRANCE
VALUE OF EXPORTS: $567.1 billion
GOODS MADE: machines and transportation equipment, airplanes, plastics
TOP CUSTOMERS: Germany, Belgium, Italy, Spain

UNITED STATES
VALUE OF EXPORTS: $1.6 trillion
GOODS MADE: soybeans, fruit, corn, chemicals, radio parts
TOP CUSTOMERS: Canada, Mexico, China, Japan

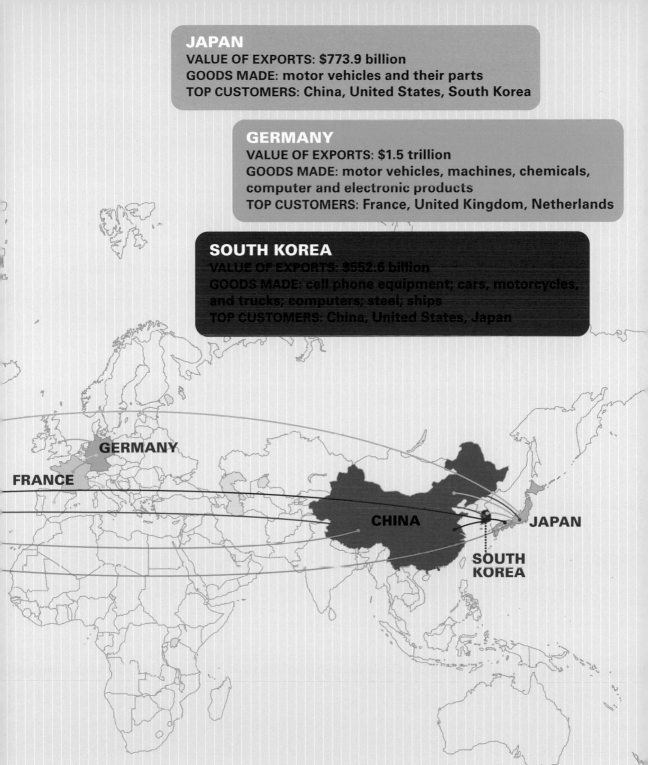

JAPAN
VALUE OF EXPORTS: $773.9 billion
GOODS MADE: motor vehicles and their parts
TOP CUSTOMERS: China, United States, South Korea

GERMANY
VALUE OF EXPORTS: $1.5 trillion
GOODS MADE: motor vehicles, machines, chemicals,
computer and electronic products
TOP CUSTOMERS: France, United Kingdom, Netherlands

SOUTH KOREA
VALUE OF EXPORTS: $552.6 billion
GOODS MADE: cell phone equipment; cars, motorcycles,
and trucks; computers; steel; ships
TOP CUSTOMERS: China, United States, Japan

GERMANY

FRANCE

CHINA

JAPAN

SOUTH
KOREA

GET TO WORK!

Not everyone has the same job. It takes many people with different jobs to make an economic system work. That's true for everything from companies to countries. Each job calls for a particular set of skills and fills a specific need within the system.

The United States has many different industries—groups of businesses that make particular products or offer specific services. Industries grow and change over time. Those changes affect the labor force—all the people in a country who are working or looking for jobs.

Take a look at the types of jobs that American workers had in 1910, 1972, and 2009. What differences do you notice?

1910

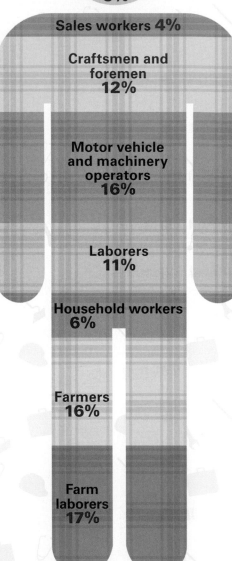

Managers, officials, and business owners
6%

Professional and technical workers
4%

Service workers 3%

Clerical workers
5%

Sales workers 4%

Craftsmen and foremen
12%

Motor vehicle and machinery operators
16%

Laborers
11%

Household workers
6%

Farmers
16%

Farm laborers
17%

1972

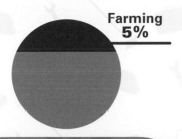

Farming
5%

Manufacturing,
transportation,
and other crafts
workers
34%

Business
managers,
professionals,
and technical
workers
22%

Sales
and
office
workers
26%

Other service
workers
13%

2009

Farming, forestry,
and fishing workers
1%

Manufacturing,
transportation,
and other
crafts workers
20%

Business
managers,
professionals,
and technical
workers
37%

Sales
and
office
workers
24%

Other
service
workers
18%

19

WORKERS ON THE MOVE

How hard is it to get a job? That depends on where you live, what jobs are available, and how many other people want them. There might be five job openings at a business. But maybe 100 people apply for those jobs. So 95 job hunters will strike out.

During the 1930s, many Americans had this problem. The United States was in the middle of the Great Depression (1929–1942), the worst economic crisis in history. People wanted to work, but there were very few jobs to go around. Then people heard about crop-picking work in California. So they migrated to California to find jobs. But it wasn't smooth sailing from there. See what happened in California as migrants flooded the workforce.

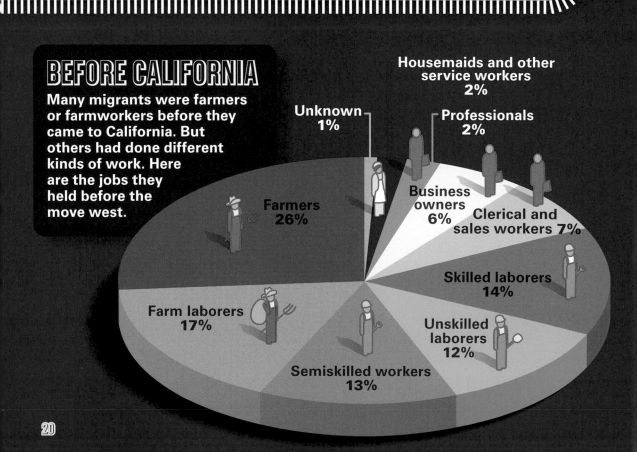

BEFORE CALIFORNIA

Many migrants were farmers or farmworkers before they came to California. But others had done different kinds of work. Here are the jobs they held before the move west.

- Farmers 26%
- Farm laborers 17%
- Semiskilled workers 13%
- Unskilled laborers 12%
- Skilled laborers 14%
- Clerical and sales workers 7%
- Business owners 6%
- Professionals 2%
- Housemaids and other service workers 2%
- Unknown 1%

About 200,000 people from Oklahoma, Texas, Colorado, Kansas, and New Mexico move west to California in the 1930s.

The migrants find that even in California, there are more laborers than there are jobs.

So many people are looking for jobs that wages (hourly pay) start to fall. People will take any jobs they can get, even if the pay is very low.

Migrants find work on large farms owned by big companies. They spend all day picking crops such as fruit or cotton. Workers make 75 cents to $1.25 a day.

Families can barely survive on the low wages. They live in shacks. They have no toilets, water, or electricity. This leads to polluted water and trash piles. Serious diseases spread quickly.

After the crops are harvested, the workers are out of jobs again. Different crops are harvested at different times, so families move from farm to farm, picking different crops.

In 1941, the United States enters World War II (1939–1945). Many migrants leave to fight in the war. Jobs are created to support the war effort. This helps strengthen the economy all around the United States.

WHAT'S THE COST?

Global economy or not, prices aren't always the same from one country to another. Your favorite pizza may be cheap where you live, but in Canada, it could cost twice as much.

A product's cost makes you think: *do I really need this?* It's important to know what is a need and what is a want. A need is something that you can't do without. A want is something you would like to have, but you don't need it to live. You *need* to eat, but maybe not that pizza.

Check out how much costs change from city to city and country to country. Depending on where you are, you may think twice about buying something you thought you needed.

BIG MAC AT MCDONALD'S

Venezuela: $9.08
Switzerland: $7.12
Canada: $5.39
United States: $4.37
Thailand: $2.92
India: $1.67

GRANDE LATTE AT STARBUCKS

Oslo, Denmark: $9.83
Moscow, Russia: $7.27
Athens, Greece: $5.84
Tokyo, Japan: $4.49
Dublin, Ireland: $4.38
New York City, New York— United States: $4.30

Costs shown for 2013 in US dollar equivalents

LARGE PAN PIZZA AT PIZZA HUT

- Toronto, Canada: $23.34
- London, United Kingdom: $22.37
- Tokyo, Japan: $21.74
- Sydney, Australia: $11.28
- New Delhi, India: $10.80
- Chicago, Illinois— United States: $10.70

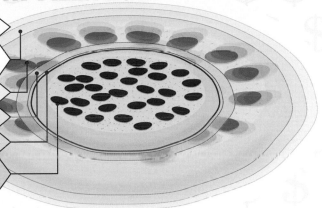

IPHONE 5S, 16GB, UNLOCKED

- Russia: $1,011.82
- France: $ 887.39
- India: $ 839.93
- South Africa: $ 819.93
- United Kingdom: $ 802.20
- United States: $ 649

MOVIE TICKET

- Mexico City, Mexico: $58.50
- Tokyo, Japan: $18.15
- London, United Kingdom: $13.72
- New York City, NY— United States: $13.00
- Moscow, Russia: $10.64
- New Delhi, India: $4.01

SEED MONEY

You go into business to make money. But to get that business started, you need to invest some money up front. Investing is spending money with the hopes of making a profit later. But what if you're broke? How can you get your business off the ground?

Time to take out a loan! A loan is borrowed money. The borrower pays the money back to the lender over a certain time. Most loans are paid back with an extra fee called interest.

Some people need just small loans—called microloans—to get their businesses up and running. These microloans change people's lives. Here's how they work:

A microloan organization receives money to make loans. The money comes from donations and repaid loans from previous borrowers.

Several people in an area decide to start businesses. The organization brings them together to form a support group. Members advise and help one another.

A borrower applies for a loan. The organization gives her between $50 and $200.

The borrower is trained by the organization. She learns how to budget her money and use computers for her business.

The borrower buys supplies to start her business. She begins to sell her products.

The organization uses the lender's money to give loans to other people. More people start businesses.

The borrower meets with her support group often. If needed, members pool their money to help her make loan payments. They also offer her business advice.

The borrower starts to make a profit. She can now save money. She can also pay back all of her loan.

JUST eCYCLE!

Think twice before you throw out that old laptop! Sure, it's slow and outdated. But it still has value—just not to you. Someone, somewhere, can find a use for it. Many products or parts of products can be recycled, restarting their journey in the world of supply and demand.

If you donate your old electronics, they can have a second life. A donation is a gift given to help others. Donating is also great for the environment. You are "eCycling" your computer, which reduces waste and reuses its materials.

See how a donated laptop has different uses and provides value to different organizations.

THE POWER OF RECYCLING

Raw materials, such as metals, are used to create the final products we buy and sell (and, sometimes, recycle). Check out how much copper, silver, and gold are in cell phones!

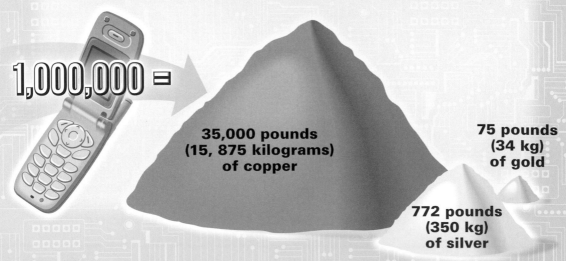

1,000,000 =

35,000 pounds (15, 875 kilograms) of copper

75 pounds (34 kg) of gold

772 pounds (350 kg) of silver

DONATE TO A CHARITY THRIFT STORE. The store takes your used laptop and sells it. The charity uses the money to help others in need.

DONATE DIRECTLY TO SOMEONE ELSE. Post the details about your laptop on a website, such as freecycle.org. Someone who needs it will come for it.

SOME PLACES TAKE OLD COMPUTERS FOR THEIR PARTS. The plastic, metal, and batteries are used to make new computers.

GIVE TO A THRIFT STORE

GIVE DIRECT

GIVE FOR PARTS

GIVE

GIVE LOCALLY

GIVE FOR REPAIR

SOME WEBSITES MATCH YOU WITH ORGANIZATIONS THAT NEED YOUR LAPTOP. Just search for the needs in your area.

DONATED LAPTOPS ARE FIXED AND THEN GIVEN TO THOSE IN NEED. The laptops may also be sold. The money may profit the company or help a charity.

A BETTER DEAL

It's the American Dream: get a job, work hard, and earn enough money to support yourself and your family. But for many working Americans, turning that dream into reality is difficult.

Before the Great Depression, many employers paid their workers very low wages. Workers could barely earn enough money to feed their families. US president Franklin D. Roosevelt came up with a plan to help struggling workers. The plan set a minimum hourly wage. Starting in 1938, employers weren't allowed to pay less than this set wage. It gave workers enough money to afford food and housing. With fairer pay, many people had a chance to improve their lives.

US law still sets a minimum hourly wage. Over the years, the wage has slowly increased as costs rise. See how the minimum wage has grown since 1938.

MAKING THE MONEY STRETCH

Why has the minimum wage gone up? Over time, many items become more expensive. In 1938, people could pay for their basic needs if they were earning $0.25 an hour. These days, that wage wouldn't be nearly enough to cover those same basic needs. Something that was worth $0.25 in 1938 would cost about $4 in modern times.

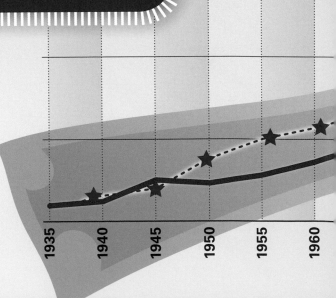

1935 1940 1945 1950 1955 1960

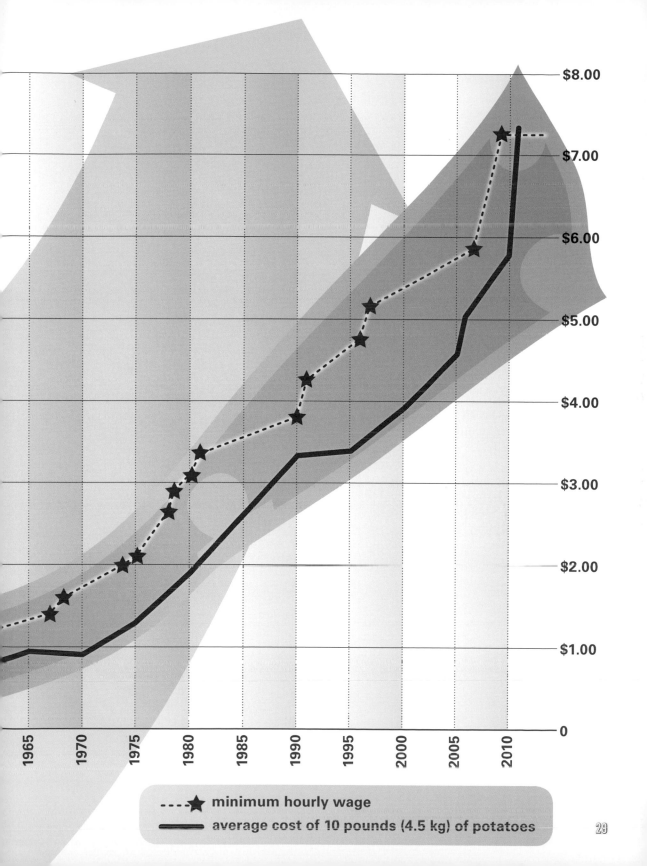

$8.00

$7.00

$6.00

$5.00

$4.00

$3.00

$2.00

$1.00

0

1965 1970 1975 1980 1985 1990 1995 2000 2005 2010

- - -★ minimum hourly wage

——— average cost of 10 pounds (4.5 kg) of potatoes

29

Glossary

ASSEMBLY LINE: a system where work is divided into small tasks and is passed from one worker to another in direct line

BARTERING: trading things, such as products or services, for other things instead of money

BENEFIT: a good result

CHARITY: an organization that raises money to help others in need

COST: the price of something, or something that is given up to get something else

CURRENCY: the form of money used by a country

DEMAND: when many people want the same item

DONATE: to give something, such as money or a computer, as a gift to help others

EXPORT: to send goods to be sold in another country

FINANCIAL: having to do with the way money is used

INDUSTRY: a group of businesses that make a product (or type of product) or provide a service

INVEST: to lend money to a person or a company in the belief that you will get more money back later

LABOR FORCE: the number of people in an area who are available for work

MIGRANT: someone who moves from place to place to do seasonal work, such as farming

PROFIT: a gain or benefit, usually involving money

RESOURCE: something or someone of value or that is useful to a company

SHORTAGE: when there is not enough of something

SUPPLY: the amount of goods or services that are needed or wanted

WAGE: the money someone is paid for a specific amount of time spent working

Further Information

Acton, Johnny, and David Goldblatt. *Economy.* New York: DK Publishing, 2010.
Learn fun facts about many aspects of the economy.

Adler, David A. *Money Madness.* New York: Holiday House, 2009.
Find out about different types of currency, how money is used around the world, and what happens to money's value when prices rise and fall.

EconEdLink
http://www.econedlink.org/interactives/economic-interactive-search.php?type=student
Check out this website for videos and games that explain key economic ideas.

Furgang, Kathy. *National Geographic Kids Everything Money.* Washington, DC: National Geographic, 2013.
Check out this book for interesting and strange facts about money—from how money is made to the money used in 1200 BCE.

Lindop, Edmund. *America in the 1930s.* Minneapolis: Twenty-First Century Books, 2010.
Find out more about life in the United States during the Great Depression.

One Hen: Microfinance for Kids
http://www.onehen.org
Visit this site to learn about how microloans work and who benefits from receiving them.

Orr, Tamra. *A Kid's Guide to the Economy.* Hockessin, DE: Mitchell Lane Publishers, 2010. Learn all about the world of finance in this book.

Reynolds, Mattie. *Saving for the Future: An Introduction to Financial Literacy.* South Egremont, MA: Red Chair Press, 2013.
Read this book to learn how to save money.

United States Mint
http://www.usmint.gov/kids
Find out more about currency with games, cartoons, fun facts, and more.

Vermond, Kira. *The Secret Life of Money: A Kid's Guide to Cash.* Toronto: Owlkids Books, 2012. Learn how money affects you—from using credit cards to the history of currency.

LERNER
e SOURCE

Expand learning beyond the printed book. Download free, complementary educational resources for this book from our website, www.lerneresource.com.

Index

PHOTO ACKNOWLEDGMENT
The background image on pp. 10–11 is used with the permission of © Alanpoulson/Dreamstime.com.